OVERCOMER

How I Survived Domestic Violence
Based on a True Story

Grace Crockett

Grace A. Crockett Books
Phoenix, AZ

ISBN-13: 978- 0-6157227-1-9
ISBN-10: 0615722717

Printed in the U.S.A.

First Edition

OVERCOMER

How I Survived Domestic Violence

Grace Crockett

Grace A. Crockett Books
Phoenix, AZ

Dedication

To all the women of the world that have overcome domestic violence situations. I decided to write this book to help other women and young ladies that struggle with "Who" they are and "Who's" they are.

To my daughter, Mercedes; my adopted daughters, Britney and Whitney; my goddaughter, Kris; and the young ladies that call me mom, Kavonne, Brandi, and Melissa.

To my sisters, Joni, Stephanie, Kim, Flora, Francis, Lora (Sissy), Teka, Shawna, my stepsister, Tanzania, and my cousin Courtney.

What is domestic violence?

Domestic violence is a pattern of behavior that includes the use or threat of violence and intimidation for the purpose of gaining power and control over another person. Violence is characterized by: Physical Abuse, Sexual Abuse, Economic Abuse, Isolation, Emotional Abuse, Control, or Verbal Abuse.

"And they overcame him because of the blood of the Lamb and because of the word of their testimony, and they did not love their life even when faced with death."

Revelation 12:11 (NASB)

Forward

Gracie,

I tell you as often as I can (just about every time we have our morning chats) how very proud I am of you. You have overcome many obstacles along the way, but look at where you are today. You know as well as I, that on a smooth road lessons are very seldom learned; it's the bumps along the way that lead to our greatest successes. Your book will inspire others as long as the reader remembers, through God ALL is possible. Keep moving forward little sis.

Already your biggest fan.

Your big sis,
Jon-Jon

Table of Contents

Introduction

In this book, *OVERCOMER,* I tell the many stories of how I was abused, and how God showed up in every situation to save me. I am blessed to be a blessing to other people that have lived their lives in fear, or full of too much pride, to get help.

I am sharing my story, my thoughts, my feelings, and where my help came from.

- Have you ever wondered what an abused person thinks about?

- How she/he must have felt during that time?

- What made them stay in a situation like that?

- Where does their help come from?

- Does pride play a big part in them not reaching out for help?

- Or is it fear that keeps them bound?

"I AM AN OVERCOMER," and you can become one, too!

Get ready to step into my world. Grab your favorite beverage, your reading glasses, and maybe a box of tissues, and prepare for a mind blowing experience.

THE EMPTY NEST

My life has been full of trials and tribulations. Misery, dilemma, and defeat are the best words to describe the worst twenty years of my life. I was lost in a world of darkness and fear. I did not have a relationship with God, even though he was always there.

As a child, I always felt I was missing something, and when I realized it was the comfort of a loving father's hugs and embrace, it was too late. As far back as I can remember my father and the father figures in my life abandoned me, either by choice or death. My biological dad was a rolling stone wherever he laid his head he called it home. He had several different women in his life and did not live in the same house as my family. Throughout my childhood, he came around only for holidays and birthdays. I can remember sitting on the couch looking out the window watching the snow fall, wishing I could see him, but he never came.

As I reminisce back to Christmas vacations during my childhood, I can say, he never showed up for Christmas. I thank God "Pops," my stepdad, was there. Lee, "Pops," came into our lives when I was around 5 years old. We were still living on 63rd and Hermitage, a few years before we moved to Altgeld Gardens. Pops was the active man in our lives; he was the man that took the place of our dad until he suffered a stroke years later.

When I turned sixteen my dad showed up at my aunt's house (with whom I was living at the time), and–as usual–I was elated to see him. Dad stayed for my birthday celebration and we spent some quiet time talking before he left. I knew when he left that evening it would be a while before I would see him again. What I didn't know was that it wouldn't be for another two years. He showed up for my high school graduation, and after the festivities he disappeared again this time for over ten years. He was not even available to give me away at my wedding.

I had been through an abusive marriage, had three children, and pregnant with my fourth before I saw my dad again. During his absence I would pray to see him and wished he was available to help me through that tough marriage. Not knowing I was a child of God and that all I needed to do was form a relationship with Him. I realized I was looking for love and acceptance in all the wrong places.

Yet to all who received him, to those who believed in his name, he gave the right to become children of God.
— (John 1:12)

THE FIRST ENCOUNTER

During the ten years I was married to my first husband I was living an unsaved life. I was partying and committing adultery. Doing all this with my husband's permission, and sometimes with his participation. I was forced to have sex with other men so that my husband can have sex with other women. I did not feel right doing this but participated in this "open relationship" because I was being obedient to my husband.

I was taught to be obedient to my husband because I was raised in the Catholic faith which does not believe in divorce. Besides, it was obey him or be beaten.

There were many incidents, but I remember the first time he hit me. The first altercation occurred because I slapped him. I do not know what provoked me to do it but I never hit him first again. This fight landed me my first black eye. Reflecting back on this relationship, I recall that at the time this incident blew my mind.

My husband, TB, had an affair with a woman by the name of Jackie. You are probably wondering how I knew...well, I'll tell you. I had a dream about him having an affair with a co-worker of mine by the name of Jackie. Jackie was a very close friend of mine and the only one at my job that knew about the abuse. I trusted Jackie and knew she was not the one he was having an affair with. But I do know that God was telling me something in that dream so when I woke up in the middle of the night I started snooping in his pockets and wallet. Ladies, be prepared for the worse when you snoop. I found a picture of a lady in his wallet with an inscription on the back, "To My Dearest Trace, with love Jackie Wright."

During a holiday weekend TB and I agreed to let his friends from Marine Security Guard battalion crash at our house. It was a typical weekend, the guys went out to the E club, and my girls and I went up to Georgetown to club hop. I got back to the house before the men folks. As I was lying in bed waiting for my husband to come home I heard a knock on the bedroom door. I answered and in walked one of his friends. He told me that Trace did not come home with them and he wanted to talk.

I did not find that unusual because all of his friends came to me for advice at one time or another. This particular friend and I were close like that. Anyway I welcomed him in my room and I sat up in the bed, and asked him what was on his mind. He asked me if I was lonely and if I wanted some company? I said we could talk so I got out the bed and we went to the den to talk. He asked me if I would consider having sex with him, and I said, "No." I asked him where was this coming from. He told me that he knew that TB was out with another woman right now and that he could make me feel good. I again turned him down and told him he was like a brother to me.

We talked for hours; until we heard the sound of birds, and looked outside and realized it was daybreak. Needless to say, TB was still not home. He showed up a few hours later and we began to argue. He did not expect me to know where he was so he started to lie. He said the only reason he went over to see her is because her boyfriend–get this–BEAT HER UP. That only made me even madder, and I have to admit, I slapped him so hard he blew his top and hit me again. But this time I called the military police (MPs) and they escorted him out of our base housing.

I stayed with him as long as I could tolerate the beatings and the adultery. I stopped allowing him to enslave me as a way to sleep with other women and decided not to live the swingers'" lifestyle anymore.

For we know that our old self was crucified with him so that the body of sin might be done away with, that we should no longer be slaves to sin. — (Romans 6:6)

The straw that broke the camel's back on this relationship was when I came home from work and found that half of our rent money was gone and my baby girl's butt the color of a red rose. I made a long awaited call to a friend and my brothers. They came with loaded guns ready for war. We loaded up my kids, a few articles of clothing, and took a ride. We never looked back.

18

SHACKING WITH THE ENEMY

Then I met someone who I thought was a great person, with good potential. We will call him RJ for sake of my identity; he threatened to kill me if he ever saw me again. RJ reminded me of a character from *Sleeping with the Enemy*. *Sleeping with the Enemy* (Twentieth Century Fox, 1991) is a psychological thriller directed by Joseph Ruben and starring Julia Roberts, as a young woman who fakes her own death in an attempt to escape her nightmarish marriage, but discovers it is impossible to elude her controlling husband (http://www.imdb.com/title/tt0102945/ accessed 10/22/12).

I can remember the first time I met him as if it was yesterday. I was working in one of the world's largest airports. One of my daily routines was to go into the employees' cafeteria and get breakfast. His smile caught my eye. My eyes were glued to those sexy lips for a few minutes before they focused on his beautiful brown eyes. RJ was a few shades darker than me, about the color of a brown paper bag. He had the sexiest body I had seen on a man in a while. He spoke with a certain swag that was unfamiliar to me. I later learned he was from Philadelphia, PA, "the city of brotherly love."

He began to flirt with me and I in turn did the same. We began to build a relationship by telephone and meeting after work. RJ confessed his love for me and I returned the term of endearment. RJ was living in a transition home for newly released prisoners. He said he had done time for selling drugs. He bragged about how much money he made and how much weight he moved in the current city we lived in. I later found out that was not the truth. Moving forward in the relationship, when RJ was released from the transitional home we decided to move in together. Mistake number one.

But fornication and all uncleanness or covetousness, let it not so much as be named among you, as becometh saints. — (Ephesians 5:3)

During the summer, his folks came to visit. We had to lie and say we were married because his grandmother was a preacher. This was far from the truth because I was still married to TB. His folks and I hit it off great; they were very nice people. The day they were leaving his grandmother pulled me to the side and handed me an envelope and told me to open it later. So out of respect I did just that.

Later that evening after we returned from the airport, RJ left the house to go do whatever he did almost every night. This time he came home more intoxicated than usual. I thought it was because he was sad to see his family go back to Philly so I was going to excuse the behavior. So to brighten his mood I decided to open the envelope in his presence, thinking it was going to make him happy. I proceed. There was a card, and I read the text and showed him the monetary gift that was inside. He began to yell saying his folks loved me more than him and accused me of taking them from him. I was so confused and stunned by his behavior that it was funny. I told him he was tripping because he was drunk. Then it started. The first hit, then the second hit, and then he knocked me to my knees.

He was punching me like he was Mike Tyson and I was Lennox Lewis. He knocked me out in 30 seconds. He continued to hit me until both my eyes were swollen and my lip was bloody. I begged him to stop, I tried to fight back, but it did not help. His punches were more powerful than mine. As he drew back his fist the last time and saw the damage he had done, he began to say he was sorry and wanted to comfort me. Comfort, really? I did not want to be near him. When I rejected his gesture to come here, he snatched me by my arm, forced me on the bed and proceeded to rape me. I laid there with his hand over my mouth, tears rolling down my face, blood streaming from my lips, with the hope that he would hurry up.

After he brutally beat and raped me, he had the nerve to fall asleep. Trembling with fear, I gathered my clothes, shoes, and keys and eased out of the room. I remember putting on my clothes in the car. I turned the key and drove out of the apartment parking lot barely able to see. I did not know where to go but I knew I had to leave before he woke up. I remember thinking if I could make it to my brother's house I would be okay. Well, I did not make it to my brother's, but I did make it to a hospital. All I remember was it was dark and lonely on the roads. I remember approaching some railroad tracks and the next thing I remember is waking up in a hospital bed, with police asking me if I knew my name. The police found me unconscious behind the wheel of my car sitting on railroad tracks. Before they could do x-rays I had to consent to a pregnancy test. The blood work was completed–and the nightmare continued–the doctor said the test was positive. At that point, I was confused, full of fear, lost, and did not know where to turn. I know that I did not what to be with RJ or relive another abusive relationship.

After I was released from the hospital a family friend moved into the apartment with me; she nursed me back to health. The morning sickness began which made me to be weak. I lay in bed for days feeling depressed and confused. I had no idea where RJ was and did not care. After I regained my strength, I moved out of the apartment and moved in with my sister and her boyfriend. I cannot remember how much time had gone by or how he found me, but RJ showed up at my sister's house. He gave his, "I'm sorry and will never hit you again," speech. Whoever told him where I was also told him I was pregnant.

My other children were in Colorado on a summer vacation with my mother and younger sister visiting one of my older sisters who lived in Pueblo. When my mom learned what happen to me she said if I stayed with RJ I would never see my kids again. So I decided to drive to Pueblo and get my kids. When RJ found out about this, he decided to steal my car. When I discovered my car was gone I reported it stolen.

He showed up the next day and begged me to let him go with me to Pueblo. I told him no, but he decided to get in the car and not get out. We took the 72-hour road trip and talked about our relationship. We planned to not fight, get married after my divorce was final, and raise the baby I was carrying.

Moving forward a few months we were settled in our own place, I started my prenatal visits, and at 13 weeks, I learned that my baby did not have a heartbeat. When he beat me that night in Atlanta, he had killed our unborn child, the doctors said the baby was dead for a while, but because the heartbeat is so faint during the early weeks, they wanted to wait until the 13th week before they declared him/her dead. I had to have surgery to have the baby taken. I was distraught for weeks after that. Every time I heard a baby cry, I began to cry and scream I want my baby back. I was all messed up in the head. Then one day we were invited to attend a church service.

RJ, the kids, and I began going to church as a family every Sunday. When I gave my testimony, the Pastor and his wife laid hands on my stomach and prayed for me. I began to except God's decision and began to read the word, attend Bible studies, and to enjoy the word of God. RJ began to resent me attending church so much and one day I came home and he beat me with my Bible and said tell God to help you out of this. After that, I stopped attending church.

He started taking the car and going out every night, sometimes not coming home until the next day. RJ and I fought more often than TB and I did. He was very aggressive and controlling. One night he was gone with my car and I was fed up with him taking my car and disappearing for days at a time. I decided to go looking for him. I called up my posse–at that point I had a few ride or die friends that I could call on for help. Anyway we went riding around Pueblo seeking to find this black bastard. I found him standing in line waiting to go into a club. I approached him and ask for the keys to the car. He told me to get out his face and stop tripping. After he noticed I was with a gang of dudes, he decided to leave. He got in the car, locked the car doors, and proceeded to drive off.

I jumped on the hood of my car and told him to get out. Can you believe this dog ass nigga drove off with me holding on to the hood? He would not stop for me to get off and entered onto a main street with me still holding on to the hood. I do not even remember how I got off the car, but the next time my nephew saw RJ he beat the crap out of him with a baseball bat.

A few days after that incident I was taking a shower and a large clot of blood feel out of me. I was rushed to the hospital where the doctors said I was just have a heavy menstrual cycle and sent me home. I continued to bleed and pass clots. The next day a clot passed about the size of a small watermelon with blood splashing all over the tub and floor of my bathroom. RJ called for an ambulance and because my pastor, even though I did not attend church regularly, had a police scanner heard my address and sent my family and a couple from church over to see what the problem was. During this hospital visit, I learned I had had a miscarriage and was so damaged inside that I would never conceive again.

My womanhood was tainted. At least that is how I felt. But, reflecting back on that season of my life now, God knew what he was doing. Not only did I have two miscarriages my divorce was denied twice.

Moving forward a few months had passed without a fight or argument. I had no love in my heart for him, only fear. All of a sudden, one evening after dinner while washing the dishes I began to pray in silence that God would remove RJ from my house and life. RJ was upstairs beginning to give the boys their bath and afterward they would have TV time with us. There was a knock on the door. He was upstairs so I answered the door, but first I called up to him to see if he was expecting company. He said no and to just it answer to see who was there. It was two white men dressed in suits and ties. They asked if RJ–by his full legal name–was home. I asked who they were and they pulled out police badges.

They came to arrest him on charges of rape and kidnapping, and needed my car for evidence. I consented to them taking my car, RJ denied the charges, and asked if they would not handcuff him in front of his kids. He cooperated with the detectives and left the house. Once outside they handcuffed him and placed him in the backset of the unmarked car. I was amazed at how fast God answered that prayer. That was the end of the relationship. I only saw RJ one more time and the night it was funny as heck.

The crew and I were hanging out, club hopping. We walked into this very popular bar and who do we see? None other than RJ himself. I was escorted by my current boyfriend who was not a punk or woman beater. RJ got in Bones' face and started to yell at him about being with is "wife," and telling me he wanted his family back. Bones was calm until RJ proceeded to raise his hand as if he was about to hit me. Bones intercepted the swing and began to whip RJ's ass. I never had a problem with RJ again other than him sending threats by others that if he could not have me he would kill me so no one would. He was convicted with rape and kidnapping a minor and taken back to prison. That was the end of that saga.

A Blessing in Disguise

Years later, I moved back to Chicago and enrolled in a computer technology school. While in class I met a guy and we started dating, not much to tell about the beginning of the relationship. We will call him LD; he was a nice, well-mannered, polite man. We did not argue or fight. LD was a peaceful, family oriented type of guy. He did not have any bad habits or hang-ups.

Well, remember in the last chapter the doctors told me that I could not bear any more children. Well that was a lie because LD and I had unprotected sex one time and I got pregnant. I later learned after I reached my seventh month that he told my younger sister he did not want any more kids of his own. This was the turning point in our relationship. He thought that I had been lying to him the entire time and that I wanted to trap him. I had no idea that I was able to conceive as I was told by doctors, and believed what I was told.

After our gift from God was born LD started to hang out with his homeboys from the hood, and began drinking and doing drugs. LD turned into a crack head over night. I know the signs because TB was a crack head. My relationship with Bones ended because he started using the crack-cocaine he had stolen from my sales inventory. That is another story entirely.

LD came home one night and accused me of sneaking someone out the back door as he was entering the front door. Cocaine makes people paranoid and imagine things. This is the night he beat me as if I stole something. I had a black eye and fat lip. It was spring break so I did not have to take the kids to school or go to work. He locked me in the room with him for days to keep me away from my kids. He was ashamed of what he did and did not want the kids to see me. After that, we had a few small spats but nothing of that magnitude. Our relationship ended because he started cheating.

One night I followed him as he went to meet up with some chick from his job. I overheard the telephone conversation he had with her as they made plans. Any way I followed them to a nasty hotel on the Southside of Chicago. I waited outside the hotel room door long enough for them to get undressed and turn off the light. Once the room went dark I knocked on the door and disguised my voice asking for a light for my cigarette. He came to the door with his boxer shorts on and when he saw it was me, he quickly shut the door. I asked for the keys to my house until he handed them over and I left. Before I left the parking lot I let all the air out of her tires. After that relationship ended, I stayed single for a while.

THE QUIET STORM

Then I met a younger man who later became my second husband. That relationship was not physically abusive at all, but it abusive in the sense that I was neglected. He spent more time with his friends and family than with me. I was the loneliest married woman in the world. I turned to other men for attention and I got it. I was a party girl, hanging out in the clubs and kicking it with my home girls. Not a good role model for the kids, I know.

This relationship was full of quiet storms. When he got mad at me he would just leave the house for days without a word. His motto was, "I can show you better than I can tell you." So when he started disappearing I started disappearing too. Anyway, this relationship lasted for 13 years and ended because he felt that I had misappropriated $20k that we both made in "the Game."

He moved on with another woman, had a kid, and till this day we are still friends. I had a lot of respect for him, just because he respected me enough not to hit me. The best thing Russ did for me is reunite me with my dad, and he was there for the kids, too. He was the best man for the job. He was the only boyfriend my kids took a liking to. They liked him so much that they began calling him dad, and to this day he is, and will always be, their "DAD." With Russ not only did my kids have an active father in their lives, but they also had another set of grandparents. My in-laws were one of the reasons I stayed with him as long as I did. His parents treated me like their own daughter. Russ was not a physical abuser, he mentally pushed me away and rejected me and made me feel worthless. After our divorce finalized I was free and back on the market, but this time it was different.

THE TRANSITION

Before my divorce was finalized, I got saved and began a relationship with the King of Kings and Lord of Lords, My Father, My God. I joined an awesome church in the west valley of Phoenix, attended Sunday, Wednesday, and bible study on Monday. I joined the singles' ministry and began to study the word of God daily. I had never had that kind of relationship before. I learned that God would never leave me nor forsake me, he will provide for me and comfort me at night. I called him my Rock.

As my faith grew my relationship got stronger. But there were hurdles that I had to cross; the road started to get bumpy. One day I decided to stop going to church and give up. I thought things would get easier when I got saved and began to learn whom I am and whose I am. Wrong. So I did not feel like fighting anymore and decided to go back to what was familiar and comfortable.

I got on the internet and began to build profiles on different dating websites. I met a few guys and started to date. I slept with a few of them but I would get this eerie feeling after each encounter. At this time I was not aware it was conviction I was experiencing. You know it really only takes a woman one time to have sex with someone and start to have feelings for him. One of the guys I had sex with took me to another level and I asked him if we could be a couple, but he said he was not ready for all that.

I missed a week of going to church and when I returned Sunday, my Pastor preached a sermon titled, "Quitting is Not an Option." At that point I knew that God was calling me back to church. Just to let you know how good God is, he revealed to me in a dream maybe a year prior, that I would be attending a mega church in the west valley, whose pastors were a young black couple. I had thought of it as just a dream. God knows I only attended, and preferred, smaller churches. Well, now I am a member of a mega church that has two locations and is in the process of opening a third location. I work in the usher ministry and love my Kingdom family. I should have known that all the other dreams and messages were for me.

But this next relationship I am about to tell you is going to blow your mind. Okay, here it goes.

Dating the Devil

I was at work one day minding my own business, taking a break away from my desk, I was on the roof walking around the track and spending time with God. I received a call on my cell phone; from an unknown number. I answered it thinking it was my son who was serving time in Iowa Department of Corrections. That is another story in itself, too. Anyway, on the other end this voice begins to speak, "Hi, you don't know me, but I just served some time with your son B-Dub, and I wanted to let you know that he has made an impact on my life. He shared his commissary with me, and we spent hours in the yard talking about God and scripture." This dude asked if we could stay in contact and I said sure. He called me every day after that; we spent hours on the phone, all most all day. Thank God for unlimited minutes.

This character was very cunning and a bible scholar, he won me over by quoting scripture. I cannot deny the fact that he is a prophet. He called me one night and told me he had a dream about me. Are you ready for this? He said he dreamed that I was raped. That I

33

was sitting in the middle of a bed, a bed that was just two mattresses on the floor, crying and when he asked me what was wrong I turned to him and said I was just raped. He said he woke up out of his sleep mad and wanted to hurt the person who did that to me. I could have said that it was only a dream, but it was the reality of my past. At that moment, I drew near to him. He became my god. What a big mistake.

He was on my mind all the time. Little signs were appearing to make me believe this man was sent by God to be my next husband. I was riding in the car with my nephew and his wife; looking out the window I read license plates as other drivers rode past. One plate read HISTHRD, the next one to pass had Iowa plates. See he lived in Iowa and in conversation, he revealed he was married two other times. I thought that was a sign. See even the devil knows the desires of your heart, so learn from me: do not be fooled.

The next few months the sermons in church were messages to me from God, but I was not hearing God at this point I was listening to my heart. I remember an Elder preached a message called, "It's Not What it Looks Like." The singles' ministry pastor preached "Don't Date the Devil," and I dismissed all those messages because I did not think they were for me. I continued the telephone conversations with dude even after I received a letter from my son who reminded me that even the devil knows the bible. He warned me that this guy was no good for me, I told him everyone has a past, and I wanted to give him a chance.

As time went on his dark side began to manifest. He would get angry and suspicious when I did not answer his calls. One night in conversation he revealed to me that his first wife committed suicide. He said he was hanging out with his friends, she called him to come home, he refused to go home, and the next morning he found her dead. He said he had been messed up from her death ever since. It seemed that he was trying to replace her with the women he kept around him. As the months moved forward and the seasons began to change, we decided it was time to meet face-to- face. So I decided to take a trip to Iowa and meet my man and spend some time with him. A week before my trip something happened that changed my life forever.

I was driving to work on March 17, 2011 and a pickup truck made a left hand turn into the intersection and t-boned my car. I was trapped inside with no feeling in my legs, confused, and angry. After I was taken to the hospital I was told that my neck was broken in two places and needed surgery. After it was all said and done I ended up with twenty-two screws and two medal plates in my neck and back. While resting after my second surgery I had a very demonic and surreal dream.

As you know images in dreams can be symbolic or just plan messages from God. In the dream I was watching from across the street as I lay on the ground unable to walk; I was paralyzed. A man and an unknown woman were getting inside a truck that was really mine, and leaving my house. He had put me out of my home and car, and began a life with this new woman. They taunted and teased me from across the street. I woke up, afraid to go back to sleep. Then I began to think that was just a nightmare because I did not own a truck. But once again God knew the beginning and end. What the devil meant for evil God always makes for good.

When I saw pictures of my car after the accident the first thing that popped into my head was a demonic force caused this. I later learned that the person who hit me, had the same last name as dude's first wife's maiden name–Hill. I think God was trying to tell me something that day; it seemed God used the connection to his wife to deliver a message. A dear friend of mine told me to end it with dude because it was a sign from God for me to avoid him and that relationship. He called me every day while I was in the hospital, talked to the doctors, nurses, and prayed with for me a speedy recovery. He was attending a little church in Dubuque, Iowa and the pastor and congregation prayed for me every service. I still thought he was sincere in his works and words. When he moved in with me and my son things were going well until he decided to chastise my son.

After that night I dreamed of killing him and I wanted him out or our lives. Dude was a huge Tupac fan and because of that he wanted to take a trip to Cali so we went for my birthday. That trip was a nightmare. I must admit I was hardheaded and not listening to the sounds of God. I learned that he was an abuser and controller. He smashed my head down in the bed one night and said, "I will break your f-ing neck if you ever try that sh** again." See, we had a tussle over my laptop that night and he wanted to break it because it would not stay connected to the internet for him to hear Tupac sing *California*. Childish, right? The next morning after he forced my head in the bed I filled a police report and got a restraining order against him.

He became history after he came to my job, stole my truck and drove it to California. When he took my new truck he took my laptop, important papers, and my first draft of this book. I continued to accept his calls because he kept promising me he was going to return my things. I was only really worried about my birth certificate, social security card, and my dad's death certificate. I searched my house high and low for weeks looking for those documents so I just know he had them. That relationship ended on September 13th, the anniversary of Tupac's death.

Even though I learned dude was crazy he still had some nice qualities. He sang to me, he wined and dined me, spoke bible, and busted my ego. He validated me; he built me up, and made me feel good about myself. But at the same time he was cocky and puffed up. I later found out he was on several different psychological medications for a few different mental disorders. He was being treated for posttraumatic stress disorder, bipolar disorder, and schizophrenia. Yeah, dude was crazy. Needless to say that relationship ended with no hope of us ever being friends.

A few months after the break up and the broken promises of returning the documents that he said, I was searching through some paperwork and discovered my birth certificate, divorce papers, and social security card tucked away in an old briefcase that I had stopped using. That was a God move. He promises the return of things taken from us.

THE FORGIVENESS TEST

This last and final chapter about a guy is not about a physical abuser, but a mental one. He had mastered the gift to manipulation and trickery. He told me all the right things to get what he wanted. One day he wrote me a text that read something like this, "I want your church to be my church, your wants to be the reason I get up in the morning, I want to be the one to run your bathwater, and massage your feet and back when they hurt. I want to be the one to tuck you in at night. I want to be your one and only man." These are the things he confessed to me–about two weeks before he disappeared.

Hound and I were introduced by two mutual friends. My friend of two years called himself hand picking this guy for me. With good intentions and my best interest at heart "E" decided to call me to see if I was interested in meeting someone. He and his girlfriend arranged a blind date for me and Hound. E thought Hound was the perfect match for me. Hound was a man that got up every day and got his grind on. He was about making his money and was not in a relationship. I met Hound two weeks before Valentine's Day.

After I arrived at my friends' apartment they discovered they had forgotten an item at the store. So E and I went to a neighborhood grocery and as we walked in the store I took notice of a well-dressed man standing near a Valentine's display with a heart shaped box of chocolates. As I stared at him I imagined he was making a perfect selection as a gift for me. E and I continued to walk past, but the finely dressed, good looking gentleman asked E, "So you just gonna walk past as if you don't see me?" E said man, "I was trying not to bring attention this way because this is Grace, my friend I wanted you to meet. Hound then replied, "Man you just spoiled the surprise." Then he extended his hand to me and introduced himself. He left the store and said now I have to go shop somewhere else.

Later at our friends' apartment Hound arrived carrying a dozen of roses and a bottle of wine to go along with the pasta dinner being prepared for us. That night we hit it off fine, and he said after he saw me in the store he thanked God for me. I shared my thoughts as I watched him in the store, we both laughed at each other's stories. We began to share more than just stories, laughter, and time, too. We became intimate and began to share our souls, we formed a soul tie. He began to tell me he loved me and I believed him and returned the words. Not sure if it was true or not but he said and I thought I was feeling it. I sometimes had this creepy feeling when I was around him. It was a time in my life that God was bringing my past in front of me to confront.

My Pastor always says, "You can't conquer something you don't confront." Forgiveness is what I was being tested on by God at this point in my life. After I had been hurt physically and mentally so many times I now did my own investigations on people I met to learn about them. I found Hound on the Internet. This guy was a member of the Bloods gang back in the day and was convicted of rape at the age of 14, and is now a registered sex offender for the rest of his life. After I learned about his past I still decided to continue being friends with him, because he did not appear to have that mindset at this stage in his life. He was always gentle, kind, and never disrespected me.

Hound and I got along fine. We communicated well and were beginning to learn each other. One evening I was over at his house and he shared with me how he respected God and knew how powerful He is. I shared with him that I had not been honest with him in the beginning. I told him that I only agreed to meet him to curve the sex crave I had going on inside me. In other words I just wanted to have sex and act like we never meet; have a one nightstand like I did in the past. What I really should have told him is that I was practicing abstinence and should have never had sex with him in the first place. Hound and I dated for six months but I did not feel right being with him because I had already given up the cookies and disrespected myself and went back on my promise to God. I decided to break all ties with him.

Hound served a purpose in my life even though we participated in the act of fornication. I allowed my flesh to overpower my spirit, but God still got the victory out of this relationship, too. Meeting Hound and making friends with him gave me the opportunity to work on the unforgiveness I had in my heart for the three men that raped me. Forgiveness is the best gift I could have given to myself. This relationship was also a test of my trust in men, which again I failed. But I thank God his mercies are new every morning. And that He turns our mourning into gladness.

THE TRUST FACTOR

So, ladies and gentlemen, as 2012 is quickly coming to an end so is my testimony. Just remember: there is a way out. Seek God, begin to fast and pray, and see the yokes begin to break and chains begin to loose. God has not given us a spirit of fear, but one of power, love, and a sound mind (2 Timothy 1:7).

Begin to set your eyes on the Lord. To be delivered you must look away from your wounds and behold the Lamb of God, for he is able to keep you from falling. Open your hearts and confess that your strength comes from the Lord. Know that you are beautifully and wonderfully made in his image. Don't let the bump in the road stop you from getting to your destination. Begin to press your way and trust in the Lord with all your heart and lean not on your own understanding; in all your ways submit to him, and he will make your paths straight (Proverbs 3:5-6).

THE PURPOSE

When I first got saved I held onto the principle that God is my Rock and foundation, and because I loved Him I should know what He has prepared for me, and it should be revealed by the Holy Spirit. I have had a desire to write a book since I was a little girl, and when my Pastor repeatedly stated many Sundays that there are books inside of us talking to the congregation I felt the Holy Spirit nudge me and say, "He is talking to you. Tell your story to help save others."

I have faced my fears and by giving my testimony I have become an overcomer. Writing this book has allowed me to boast about my troubles and has given purpose to my pain. I thank God for the Judas' that kissed me, and I stopped cursing my crises and stop resisting and let go. This experience has allowed me to transition and get in alignment with God and ride out what he told me, "The darkness I will bring to light." The book was to bring me to my place of knowing who I am and whose I am. And to know that God created me perfectly and wonderfully; I am an unrepeated miracle, I am ministry material, I am fine flour that has been processed like wheat.

The Answers

Have you ever wondered what an abused person thinks about?

A way out, by any means necessary. I thought of suicide, murder, and running away into hiding.

How she/he must have felt during that time?

Fear, plain and simple. I was so afraid of my own mind. I did not want to think for myself or speak for myself. Afraid if I said the wrong thing or did the opposite of what he wanted I would be hit.

What made them stay in a situation like that?

I was told that no one would want a fat ass with three kids. I was afraid to leave.

Where does their help come from?

My help came from God.

Does pride play a big part in them not reaching out for help?

Yes, no one wants to tell people they are allowing their mate to beat them.

Or is it fear that keeps them bound?

Both fear and pride are responsible for us not leaving. We must set aside our prideful was and allow God to bring help our way. The best way to overcome a situation is to face it.

One in every four women will experience domestic violence in her lifetime.

Most cases of domestic violence are never reported to the police.

The Facts

From: "Violence by Intimates: Analysis of Data on Crimes by Current or Former Spouses, Boyfriends, and Girlfriends, U.S. Department of Justice (March, 1998)"

- Estimates range from 960,000 incidents of violence against a current or former spouse, boyfriend, or girlfriend each year to 4 million women who are physically abused by their husbands or live-in partners each year.

- While women are less likely than men to be victims of violent crimes overall, women are 5 to 8 times more likely than men to be victimized by an intimate partner.

- Violence by an intimate partner accounts for about 21% of violent crime experienced by women and about 2 % of the violence experienced by men.

- 31,260 women were murdered by an intimate from 1976-1996.

- Females accounted for 39% of the hospital emergency department visits for violence-related injuries in 1994 but 84% of the persons treated for injuries inflicted by intimates.

- The National Domestic Violence Hotline has received more than 700,000 calls for assistance since February 1996. Source: National Domestic Violence Hotline, December, 2001.

- It is estimated that 503,485 women are stalked by an intimate partner each year in the United States. Source: National Institute of Justice, July 2000.

- Studies show that child abuse occurs in 30-60% of family violence cases that involve families with children. Source: "The overlap between child maltreatment and woman battering." J.L. Edleson, Violence Against Women, February, 1999.

- Nearly one-third of American women (31 percent) report being physically or sexually abused by a husband or boyfriend at some point in their lives. Source: Commonwealth Fund survey, 1998.

- About 75% of the calls to law enforcement for intervention and assistance in domestic violence occur after separation from batterers. One study revealed that half of the homicides of female spouses and partners were committed by men after separation from batterers (Barbara Hart, Remarks to the Task Force on Child Abuse and Neglect, April 1992).

- Each year, medical expenses from domestic violence total at least $3 to $5 billion. Businesses forfeit another $100 million in lost wages, sick leave, absenteeism and non-productivity. Source: Domestic Violence for Health Care Providers, 3rd Edition, Colorado Domestic Violence Coalition, 1991.

- From 1983 to 1991, the number of domestic violence reports received increased by almost 117%. Source: New York State Division of Criminal Justice Services, 1983 and 1991.

- Violence is the reason stated for divorce in 22% of middle-class marriages. Source: EAP Digest November/December 1991.

- Every year, domestic violence results in almost 100,000 days of hospitalizations, almost 30,000 emergency department visits, and almost 40,000 visits to a physician. Source: American Medical Association. 5 issues American Health. Chicago 1991.

- Studies by the Surgeon General's office reveal that domestic violence is the leading cause of injury to women between the ages of 15 and 44, more common than automobile accidents, muggings, and cancer deaths combined. Other research has found that half of all women will experience some form of violence from their partners during marriage, and that more than one-third are battered repeatedly every year. Source: Journal of American Medical Association, 1990.

- Battered women seek medical attention for injuries sustained as a consequence of domestic violence significantly more often after separation than during cohabitation; about 75% of the visits to emergency rooms by battered women occur after separation (Stark and Flitcraft, 1988).

- Women who leave their batterers are at 75% greater risk of severe injury or death than those who stay. Source: Barbara Hart, National Coalition Against Domestic Violence, 1988.

- It is estimated that 25% of workplace problems such as absenteeism, lower productivity, turnover and excessive use of medical benefits are due to family violence. (Employee Assistance Providers/MN)

- In 92% of all domestic violence incidents, crimes are committed by men against women. Source: "Violence Against Women", Bureau of Justice Statistics, U.S. Department of Justice, January, 1994.

- Of women who reported being raped and/or physically assaulted since the age of 18, three quarters (76 percent) were victimized by a current or former husband, cohabitating partner, date or boyfriend. Source: "Prevalence Incidence, and Consequences of Violence Against Women: Findings from the National Violence Against Women Survey", U.S. Department of Justice, November, 1998.

- In 1994, women separated from their spouses had a victimization rate 1 1/2 times higher than separated men, divorced men, or divorced women. Source: "Sex Differences in Violent Victimization", 1994, U.S. Department of Justice, September, 1997.

- In 2003, among all female murder victims in the U.S., 30% were slain by their husbands or boyfriends. Source: Uniform Crime Reports of the U.S. 1996, Federal Bureau of Investigation, 2003 (January - June).

- A child exposed to the father abusing the mother is at the strongest risk for transmitting violent behavior from one generation to the next. Source: "Report of the American Psychological Association Presidential Task Force on Violence and the Family", APA, 1996.

- Forty percent of teenage girls age 14 to 17 report knowing someone their age who has been hit or beaten by a boyfriend. Source: Children Now/Kaiser Permanente poll, December, 1995.

- Family violence costs the nation from $5 to $10 billion annually in medical expenses, police and court costs, shelters and foster care, sick leave, absenteeism, and non-productivity. Source: Medical News, American Medical Association, January, 1992.

- Husbands and boyfriends commit 13,000 acts of violence against women in the workplace every year. Source: "Violence and Theft in the Workplace", U.S. Department of Justice, July, 1994.

- The majority of welfare recipients have experienced domestic abuse in their adult lives and a high percentage are currently abused. Source: Trapped by Poverty, Trapped by Abuse: New Evidence Documenting the Relationship Between Domestic Violence and Welfare, The Taylor Institute, April, 1997.

- One in five female high school students reports being physically or sexually abused by a dating partner. Source: Massachusetts Youth Risk Behavior Survey (YRBS), August 2001.

Relationship Quiz

How is your relationship?

Does your partner:

- Embarrass you with bad names and put-downs?
- Look at you or act in ways that scare you?
- Control what you do, who you see or talk to, or where you go?
- Stop you from seeing or talking to friends or family?
- Take your money or Social Security check, make you ask for money, or refuse to give you money?
- Tell you you're a bad parent or threaten to take away or hurt your children?
- Make all the decisions?
- Act like the abuse is no big deal, it's your fault, or even deny doing it?
- Destroy your property or threaten to kill your pets?
- Intimidate you with guns, knives, or other weapons?
- Shove you, slap you, or hit you?
- Force you to drop charges?
- Threaten to commit suicide?
- Threaten to kill you?

If you checked even one, you may be in an abusive relationship. Seek help from your local Coalition against Domestic Violence or your local church.

About the Author

Grace A. Crockett, MBA, is the founder of Agnes' Centers for Domestic Solutions. Grace obtained her Master of Business Administration from the University of Phoenix in 2011. She is inspired by the word of God, which speaks very clearly to her. Grace is a mother of four biological children, and 10 foster children. She enjoys serving as an usher in her local church while learning the gospel and building her relationship with God.

Visit Agnes' Centers for Domestic Solutions at http://www.agnescenters.com.